The Story of

CIVIL RIGHTS HERO

JOHN LEWIS

by **Jim Haskins and Kathleen Benson**

additional material by
Kathleen Benson

with illustrations by
Aaron Boyd

Lee & Low Books Inc.
New York

In loving memory of Jim Haskins — K.B.

For Jan, you made me better — A.B.

Text from *John Lewis in the Lead: A Story of the Civil Rights Movement* copyright © 2006 by Kathleen Benson

Sidebar text by Kathleen Benson copyright © 2018 by Lee & Low Books Inc.

Illustrations by Aaron Boyd copyright © 2018 by Lee & Low Books Inc.

Photo credits: p. 12: Library of Congress, Prints & Photographs Division, FSA/OWI Collection, LC-DIG-fsa-8a23316. Photograph by Russell Lee • p. 13: Library of Congress, Prints & Photographs Division, FSA/OWI Collection, LC-DIG-fsa-8b29588. Photograph by Dorothea Lange • p. 17: © World History Archive / age fotostock • p. 19: © World History Archive / age fotostock • p. 25: courtesy Everett Collection • p. 26: public domain • p. 27: courtesy Everett Collection • p. 33: The George F. Landegger Collection of Alabama Photographs in Carol M. Highsmith's America, Library of Congress, Prints and Photographs Division, LC-DIG-highsm-0728 • p. 47: Steve Eberhardt / ZUMA Wire / Alamy Live News

LEE & LOW BOOKS Inc.
95 Madison Avenue
New York, NY 10016
leeandlow.com

Edited by Louise May and Cheryl Klein
Book design by Abhi Alwar and Charice Silverman
Book production by The Kids at Our House

The text is set in Vollkorn.
The display font is set in Avenir.
The illustrations are rendered in ink and watercolor.

10 9 8 7 6 5 4 3 2 1
First Edition

Cataloging-in-Publication Data
Names: Haskins, James, 1941-2005, author. | Benson, Kathleen, author. | Boyd, Aaron, 1971- illustrator.
Title: The story of civil rights hero John Lewis / by Jim Haskins and Kathleen Benson ; additional material by Kathleen Benson ; with illustrations by Aaron Boyd.
Other titles: John Lewis in the lead
Description: New York : Lee & Low Books Inc. , 2018. | "Text from John Lewis in the Lead: A Story of the Civil Rights Movement, 2006." | Includes bibliographical references.
Identifiers: LCCN 2018040714 | ISBN 9781620148549 (pbk. : alk. paper)
Subjects: LCSH: Lewis, John, 1940 February 21---Juvenile literature. | Legislators--United States--Biography--Juvenile literature. | African American legislators--Biography--Juvenile literature. | United States. Congress. House--Biography--Juvenile literature. | Civil rights workers--United States--Biography--Juvenile literature. | African American civil rights workers--Biography--Juvenile literature. | Student Nonviolent Coordinating Committee (U.S.)--Biography--Juvenile literature. | African Americans--Civil rights--Juvenile literature. | Civil rights movements--Southern States--History--20th century--Juvenile literature.
Classification: LCC E840.8.L43 H37 2018 | DDC 328.73/092 [B] --dc23
LC record available at https://lccn.loc. gov/2018040714

TABLE OF CONTENTS

CHAPTER ONE
WALKING WITH THE WIND

John Lewis was born at a time when the winds of change were blowing, just waiting for someone to catch them and hold on long enough for everyone to feel the breeze.

It was another wind altogether that blew one day when John was a little boy. He was playing in the dirt yard of his Aunt Seneva's house with many of his brothers, sisters, and cousins. The sky began to cloud over and the wind started to pick up. In the distance lightning flashed. Then came a loud clap of thunder and a **torrent** of rain.

"Come inside quick, children," said Aunt Seneva, and she **hustled** them all into her small wooden house.

Inside, Aunt Seneva and the children huddled together, hushed, listening to the wind howl and feeling the house shake. Suddenly they felt the floor move. The wind was so strong it lifted a corner of the house, trying to pull it into the sky.

Aunt Seneva started to cry, and the children began to sob too. Then Aunt Seneva gathered her courage. "Everybody hold hands!" she called, and the frightened children did as they

were told. "Now, we got to walk over to that corner." They hurried to the corner, and the combined weight of their bodies settled the house back down.

Soon another corner began to lift from the force of the wind, so they rushed to that corner. Each time the wind lifted part of the house, Aunt Seneva and the children held it down. Holding hands, they walked with the wind until the danger had passed.

The storm didn't last long, but John never forgot that day.

CHAPTER TWO

LEARNING TO PREACH

In 1945, when John turned five, he was put in charge of his family's chickens. He had to take care of about sixty animals on the farm near Troy, Alabama, where his family lived as sharecroppers. They worked on a white man's land in return for a place to live and a share of the crops they grew.

John was happy and proud to have this job. He liked chickens and took his responsibility very seriously. He carried buckets of feed to the hen-house. He kept it clean. He named each chicken. Two of his favorites were Big Belle and L'il Pullet.

At night, to quiet the chickens, John preached to them. He wanted to be a minister, and this was a good way to practice. John's habit of giving sermons in the chicken coop earned him the nickname Preacher.

During the time John was growing up, the South was **segregated**. Black people were kept apart from white people. It was against the law for blacks to eat in white restaurants. Black children could not go to the same schools as white children. Black people had to sit in the backs of public buses and give up their seats to whites if the "white seats" in the front were filled.

John realized that segregation was keeping his family from having a better life. This made him angry, but his parents warned John to stay quiet. "Don't get in trouble," they said. "Don't get in the way."

One day when he was fifteen, John heard Dr. Martin Luther King, Jr., on the radio. Dr. King was a preacher in Montgomery, Alabama, and he was talking about the bus **boycott**. Black people in Montgomery had stopped riding the buses to protest bus segregation. When Dr. King said segregation was wrong, John felt as though Dr. King were speaking directly to him, telling him it was time to get in the way. It was time to turn things upside down in order to set them right side up.

Sharecropping

Before the Civil War, the southern agricultural **economy** was based on slave labor. After the war ended, cash was in short supply, and the owners of large **plantations** could not afford to pay workers to plant and harvest hundreds of acres of crops. The former slaves had no place to live and no way to make a living. One answer to this **dilemma** was sharecropping. Under this system, a large landowner leased plots of land to families, both black and white, who farmed the land in exchange for a share of the crops they grew. Many formerly enslaved people—now called *freedmen* and *freedwomen*—became sharecroppers on the same plantations where they had lived as slaves before the war.

This system was good for the freedmen because they could work the land with their families. But there were many **drawbacks** to sharecropping. The land and any buildings on it belonged to the landlord. So did the farm animals and the tools. Even though the sharecropper was supposed to keep a portion of the crops, by the time he finished harvesting, he would have little left for himself and his family. In years of floods or drought, the sharecropper wouldn't even have enough crops to sell to pay his debts. The system did not change until the 1930s and 1940s, when sharecroppers **unionized**, new farm machinery required fewer people to work the land, and many African Americans left the South for opportunities elsewhere.

This May 1938 photo shows a sharecropper's cabin in southeast Missouri, standing in a cotton field ruined by hail.

John Lewis recalled, "Even a six-year-old could tell that this sharecropper life was nothing but a bottomless pit. I watched my father sink deeper and deeper into debt, and it broke my heart. More than that, it made me angry. There was no way to get ahead with this kind of farming. The best you could do was do it well enough to keep doing it. That looked like no kind of life to me, and I didn't keep my opinion to myself. Early on, to the **dismay** of the rest of my family, I would speak out against what we were doing right there in the fields."

The child of an Alabaman sharecropping family works a field in July 1936.

CHAPTER THREE
GETTING IN THE WAY

Inspired by Dr. King, John took his first steps to protest segregation. He asked for a library card at his county public library, knowing that black people were not allowed to have cards. John was not surprised that the librarian said the library was for whites only. Then he went home and wrote the library a letter of protest.

After graduating from high school in 1957, John went to Nashville, Tennessee, to study to become a minister. He wrote to Dr. King, who invited John to visit him in Montgomery. When they met, Dr. King said they could fight the **injustice** of segregation peacefully. He told John to study the life of Mohandas K. Gandhi, who had led nonviolent protests in India.

John liked Gandhi's idea of nonviolent resistance as a way to bring about social change. With this in mind, John organized **sit-ins** at lunch counters where blacks were not allowed to eat with whites. In 1961 he joined the Student Nonviolent Coordinating Committee (SNCC). The students went on **Freedom Rides** to challenge segregation at interstate bus terminals. Blacks and whites sat next to each other on buses that traveled from state to state.

John's commitment to nonviolence would soon be tested. In May 1961 a bus carrying John and other Freedom Riders arrived at the Montgomery, Alabama, bus station. John was the first one off the bus. Aside from a group of newspaper reporters, the streets were strangely deserted. John had just begun to deliver a statement to the reporters when suddenly hundreds of white people came running from behind buildings and around corners. Waving baseball bats, boards, bricks, tire irons, hoes, and rakes, they screamed out insults.

"Let's all stand together," John cried, as the mob attacked the Freedom Riders. Someone hit John on the head with a wooden crate, and he fell to the ground. After being treated at a local hospital, John was **anxious** to rejoin his group and carry on.

The brutal attack was big news, and Dr. King was concerned. He rushed to Montgomery and tried to convince John to protect himself and stop the rides, but John would not. So with a bandaged and bruised John Lewis at his side, Dr. King held a press conference to announce that the Freedom Rides would continue.

Mohandas K. Gandhi

John Lewis followed Martin Luther King, Jr., in adopting the ideas of nonviolent resistance from an Indian leader named Mohandas K. Gandhi. Gandhi is credited with leading the people of India to independence from Great Britain.

Gandhi was born in India in 1869. At the time, Indian society was separated into many different classes. The lower classes were badly treated and had few rights.

Gandhi as a lawyer in South Africa, 1905.

As a young lawyer, Gandhi traveled to South Africa to handle an Indian merchant's case. In South Africa, which was also ruled by Great Britain, he found a racially segregated society in which Indians were treated almost as badly as native black South Africans. He came to understand that a social class system is wrong wherever it occurs.

Gandhi believed that British **colonial** rule was to blame for the injustices in both South Africa and India. He decided that the only way for India to gain independence from Great Britain was for Indians to unite across class lines and to engage together in **passive resistance** against British rule. He eventually chose the word "satyagraha" to describe his vision of how he wanted his people to resist the British. It is a combination of two **Sanskrit** words: *satya*, which means "truth" and can imply firm love, and *agraha*, which could mean force. Those who practice satyagraha try not to engage in violence in any form, to the extent that they will not even defend themselves against physical attack.

After he returned to India, Gandhi chose to put aside his upper-middle-class suits and dress in a simple **loincloth**. He led many nonviolent protests against British rule, including **fasting** and boycotts, and was arrested and jailed countless times. Whenever his followers turned to violence, he would refuse to eat until they stopped. Eventually, those who had reacted with violence were persuaded by Gandhi's "truth force." He became known as the *Mahatma*, which means "the great-souled one."

Gandhi encouraged the people of India to boycott foreign-made textiles and buy Indian goods instead. In this 1945 photo, he spins yarn for cloth using traditional methods.

It took thirty years, but in 1947 Gandhi's "truth force" movement succeeded in winning India's independence from Great Britain.

CHAPTER FOUR

THE MARCH ON WASHINGTON

Over the next two years, John led many protests. He was often beaten and arrested, but he did not give up. He believed segregation was unjust. He was committed to bringing people together to fight for their **civil rights**.

In August 1963 John, as the head of SNCC, was invited to speak at the March on Washington for Jobs and Freedom. The gathering was intended to make Congress pass a civil rights bill that would guarantee equal rights for black people.

At age twenty-three, John Lewis was the youngest of the six civil rights leaders who spoke in front of the Lincoln Memorial on the **National Mall**. He was also the most outspoken.

He had planned to give a **fiery** speech, but the five older leaders persuaded him to tone it down. Nevertheless, his speech was memorable for its forcefulness, as **excerpted** here:

. . . To those who have said, "Be patient and wait," we have long said that we cannot be patient. We do not want our freedom gradually, but we want to be free now! We are tired. We are tired of being beaten by policemen. We are tired of seeing our people locked up in jail over and over again. And then you holler, "Be patient." How long can we be patient? We want our freedom and we want it now. We do not want to go to jail. But we will go to jail if this is the price we must pay for love, brotherhood, and true peace.

I appeal to all of you to get into this great revolution that is sweeping this nation. Get in and stay in the streets of every city, every village and **hamlet** of this nation until true freedom comes, until the revolution of 1776 is complete. We must get in this revolution and complete the revolution. For in the Delta in Mississippi, in southwest Georgia, in the **Black Belt of Alabama**, in Harlem, in Chicago, Detroit, Philadelphia, and all over this nation, the black masses are on the march for jobs and freedom.

They're talking about slow down and stop. We will not stop. . . . If we do not get meaningful legislation out of this Congress, the time will come when we will not confine our marching to Washington. We will march through the South; through the streets of Jackson, through the streets of Danville, through the streets of Cambridge, through the streets of Birmingham. But we will march with the spirit of love and with the spirit of **dignity** that we have shown here today. By the force of our demands, our determination, and our numbers, we shall splinter the segregated South into a thousand pieces and put them together in the image of God and democracy. We must say: "Wake up, America! Wake up!" For we cannot stop, and we will not and cannot be patient.

After John spoke, Dr. King delivered his famous "I Have a Dream" speech, expressing the hope that one day all Americans would be free to enjoy equal rights and opportunities.

The March on Washington had an impact. The following year President Lyndon B. Johnson signed the Civil Rights Act of 1964, making racial **discrimination** in restaurants, bus stations, and other public places illegal and requiring equal employment opportunities for all citizens.

John now turned his attention to voters' rights. With his help, SNCC made plans to register southern black people to vote. It would be a hard task. Many white people could not bear the thought of black people having the freedom to vote. They felt threatened, and feared that blacks would gain political power over them.

Student Nonviolent Coordinating Committee

On Monday, February 1, 1960, four students from North Carolina Agricultural & Technical College, an all-black school, sat down at a whites-only lunch counter in Greensboro, North Carolina. They were refused service and the store manager asked them to leave, which they did. The following day, the students returned, joined by twenty-five others. By Thursday, students from a nearby college for white women had joined the protesters, and by Saturday, fourteen hundred student protesters were sitting in at or **picketing** Greensboro's segregated stores. By the end of February, many stores had either begun to serve black customers or closed down.

The student protest movement spread across the South. **Ella Baker**, who worked with Dr. King's **Southern Christian Leadership Conference (SCLC)**, was excited about this development and left the SCLC to

Ella Baker, circa 1944.

organize activist students. She called a meeting at Shaw University in Raleigh, NC, on Easter weekend in April 1960. The participants in the meeting formed the Student Nonviolent Coordinating Committee (SNCC).

 The new organization adopted as its symbol a picture of a white hand shaking a black hand because the students believed that both races could work together for equality for black people.

SNCC members engaged in Freedom Rides, voter registration drives, and all of the other major nonviolent protests of the Civil Rights Movement. John Lewis was the third president of SNCC, elected in June 1963. As such, he was one of the six civil rights leaders who spoke at the 1963 March on Washington, later known as the **"Big Six."**

By the late 1960s, however, many members of SNCC were tired of the slow pace of nonviolent protest. John Lewis was voted out as president in May 1966, and SNCC began to focus less on nonviolent protest and more on demanding equal rights. The new

Members of SNCC and the Congress of Racial Equality (CORE) chain themselves to a federal courthouse in New York City to protest civil rights abuses in Mississippi, 1965.

leader of SNCC, **Stokely Carmichael**, is credited with originating the term "Black Power!" in 1966. In 1969, the members voted to change the word "Nonviolent" in its name to "National," signaling a major split with the nonviolent Civil Rights Movement. SNCC became inactive after the early 1970s.

CHAPTER FIVE
TROUBLE IN SELMA

In January 1965 John went to Selma, Alabama. More than fifteen thousand black adults were **eligible** to vote in the county where Selma was located, but only about three hundred were registered. John and other SNCC workers began leading groups of people to the city courthouse in Selma to register to vote. Each time a group arrived, the clerk hung up a sign that read OUT TO LUNCH. It didn't matter what time of day they arrived. The sign always went up.

The groups waited outside the courthouse without complaint, hour after hour, all day long. People grew tired. Their feet hurt. But they remained dignified and calm. John encouraged them, praising their courage to endure the boredom as well as the threat of violence.

Jim Clark, the sheriff of Selma, was

determined not to let blacks register to vote. When he realized they would continue to wait to enter the courthouse, Sheriff Clark ordered his officers to block the entrance. During three days of peaceful protests, more than two hundred people were arrested, including John.

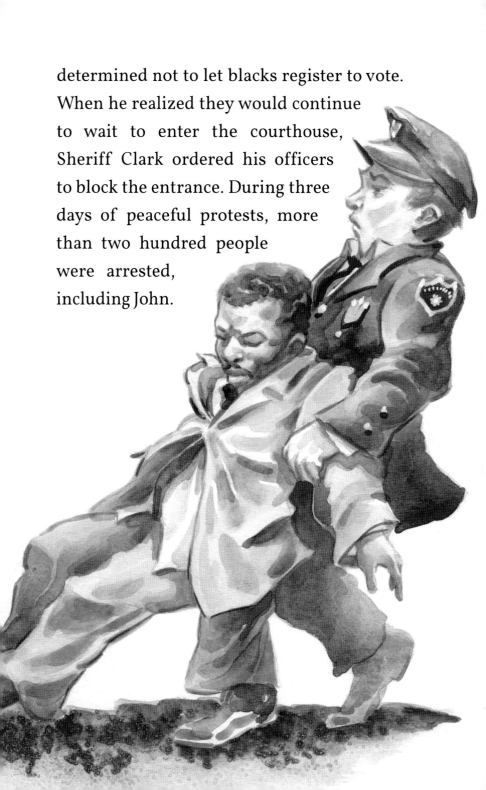

One night after a rally to support people trying to register to vote in Marion, a city near Selma, a group started marching to the courthouse. Suddenly the streetlights went out and police began attacking the marchers. To seek safety, a woman and her son ran into a small cafe. A policeman started hitting the woman, and her son, Jimmie Lee Jackson, was shot as he tried to protect her. He died soon after.

John was heartbroken when he heard the news. People had been beaten, arrested, and jailed during their protests, but no one had been killed until now.

Hundreds of people crowded into the church to hear Dr. King preach at Jimmie Lee Jackson's funeral. Afterward, John walked with Dr. King and a thousand other mourners to the graveyard. Along the way someone suggested that they keep walking right to Montgomery, the state capital, and deposit the casket on the capitol steps. Jimmie was buried in Marion that day, but back in Selma many people liked the idea of a march to Montgomery.

Montgomery was fifty-four miles from Selma. Fear mixed with excitement at the idea of a march that would take about five days. There were also rumors that Alabama governor George Wallace would let state troopers do whatever was necessary to prevent the Selma-to-Montgomery march. Dr. King was supposed to lead the marchers, but after receiving threats on his life, he asked his close ally, the Reverend **Hosea Williams**, to take his place.

The Black Church and the Civil Rights Movement

Black churches have long played a major role in African American life, dating back to slavery times. Most black churches are either Baptist or Methodist, because as far back as the 1700s, white Baptists and Methodists reached out to enslaved Africans to convert them to their beliefs. The Methodist Church even licensed black preachers. The first independent black congregation, Bethel African Methodist Episcopal Church, was organized in the North, in Philadelphia, PA, in 1787. The first independent black congregation in the South, First African Baptist, was organized in Savannah, GA, in 1790. Besides providing a place for black people to pray without having to be segregated in upstairs balconies or back pews, these churches served as community centers, self-help organizations, and social centers.

During the Civil Rights Movement, black churches often served as movement headquarters, hosting meetings, getting the word out about planned protests, and encouraging their congregations in the nonviolent fight for their rights. Most of the major leaders in the Civil Rights Movement were Baptist ministers: Martin Luther King, Jr.; his associates in the SCLC, **Ralph David Abernathy**, **Andrew Young**, and **Wyatt Tee Walker**; and **James Farmer**, founder of the **Congress of Racial Equality**. John Lewis was also a Baptist minister.

Brown Chapel African Methodist Episcopal Church in Selma, AL, played a particularly important role in the movement. It served as the headquarters of the SCLC for the first three months of 1965, when that organization planned and carried out two marches from Selma to Montgomery, and it was the starting point for both. First Baptist Church, another black church in Selma, served as the headquarters for SNCC, which launched the Selma voting rights campaign that led to the marches. Both churches are located on what has been renamed Martin Luther King, Jr. Street. Brown Chapel AME Church is now a National Historic Landmark.

Brown Chapel AME Church.

CHAPTER SIX

ON THE BRIDGE

Late in the afternoon on Sunday, March 7, 1965, John Lewis and Reverend Williams stood at the head of a group of nearly six hundred people. From Brown Chapel AME Church they marched down Sylvan Street, turned right on Water Street, then walked to Broad Street. There they turned left and headed up the steep western arch of the Edmund Pettus Bridge, which led out of Selma. Several dozen of Sheriff Clark's men watched the marchers as they passed.

At the crest of the bridge, John suddenly saw a sea of state troopers spread out across the highway. On either side and behind them were more of Sheriff Clark's men, some riding horses.

The commander of the troopers, Major John Cloud, raised his **bullhorn**. "This is an unlawful assembly," he boomed. "You are ordered to **disperse** and go back to your church or your homes."

John stood at the top of the bridge. Ahead of him was the swarm of state troopers. Below him swirled the brown water of the river. All around were crowds of screaming, jeering people, their faces **contorted** with hate. And behind him were hundreds of courageous but frightened black marchers—mothers and fathers, teenagers and teachers, beauticians and undertakers, farmers and mechanics.

Again, Major Cloud raised the bullhorn to his lips. "You have two minutes to turn around and go back to your church," he shouted.

John believed that everyone should have the right to vote and that they should not back down.

But he saw they were trapped. They could not turn around—there were too many people on the bridge. They could not go forward either. That was inviting an attack by the state troopers. John could feel the marchers begin to panic. He knew they were waiting for him to tell them what to do.

Standing at the crest of the Edmund Pettus Bridge, John remembered the way his Aunt Seneva had taught him to walk with the wind. He remembered that people can survive any storm if they stick together.

"We should pray together," John told Reverend Williams. The reverend was thinking much the same thing. He asked Major Cloud if they could have a moment to pray.

Just as those at the front of the march bowed their heads, and just one minute after Major Cloud's two-minute warning, Cloud gave the order to attack. A wave of state troopers charged up the bridge. His head bowed in prayer, John heard the sounds of terror—the pounding of horses' hooves and troopers' heavy boots, the shouts and screams of men and women, the cries of frightened people trying to pray and be brave.

Suddenly a trooper swung his club at John, knocking him to the ground. John tried to protect his head as the trooper hit him again.

Other marchers at the front of the group took blows too. Those behind them turned to go back, but there were so many people on the bridge it was hard to move. As the marchers tried to get away from the troopers, they were attacked by more of Sheriff Clark's men. The mob also attacked cameramen and reporters, but they couldn't stop them from reporting the violence. The pictures and television broadcasts of state troopers and policemen beating defenseless people brought the country face-to-face with the riot that would soon be known as Bloody Sunday.

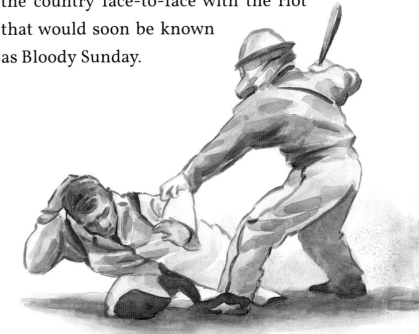

Although John was badly injured, he somehow made it back to Brown Chapel that night. The church and surrounding area were filled with people protesting what had happened on the bridge. John managed to speak to the crowd, and he asked President Johnson to protect the marchers, whose only desire was to register to vote. Then John allowed himself to be taken to the hospital.

John had a serious head injury, a **concussion**. In the hospital, his feelings of helplessness were as bad as the physical pain. He didn't know what was going on outside. He didn't know what had happened to the people on the bridge.

Finally reports began to trickle in. Bloody Sunday was a national scandal. There were demonstrations in more than eighty cities against the brutality of the Alabama police and troopers. There were calls for a federal law that would guarantee everyone the right to vote. By the time John was released from the hospital, he had real hope that black people would soon have the same voting rights as whites.

John joined with Dr. King and other civil rights leaders to show Alabama and the nation that they would not give up. A new date, Sunday, March 21, was set for a march from Selma to Montgomery. Word soon came that religious leaders, elected officials, celebrities, and ordinary people from across the country planned to join the march in support of voting rights for all Americans.

This time, under the protection of federal troops, more than three thousand people started out from Selma. Over five days the sun burned down on the marchers and rain fell in torrents, but no one complained, no one gave up. "We felt bonded with one another, with the people we passed, with the entire nation," John recalled. By the time the marchers reached Montgomery, they were twenty-five thousand strong.

Five months later President Johnson signed the Voting Rights Act of 1965, which protected the rights of all Americans to vote. The act made it a crime to use force against anyone trying to register and vote.

CHAPTER SEVEN

JOHN LEWIS IN CONGRESS

Over the next two decades, John Lewis continued to work for civil rights and fairer, stronger communities for everyone. He served as the director of a national volunteer organization and as a member of the city council of Atlanta, Georgia.

In 1986, twenty-one years after the Voting Rights Act, the votes of both black and white citizens elected John Lewis to the United States House of Representatives, where he continues to serve today, representing Georgia's 5th **Congressional District**. The 5th CD includes most of Georgia's state capital, Atlanta, plus parts of Fulton, DeKalb, and Clayton Counties. Members of Congress (also known as the US

House of Representatives) must run for re-election every two years, so Congressman Lewis has been reelected fifteen times since he first won the seat in November 1986. Only once in all that time did he fail to win at least 70 percent of all votes. In four elections—1996, 2004, 2006, and 2008—he ran unopposed, meaning that no one ran against him.

Much of Congress's work is done through committees. When John Lewis first went to Congress, he served on the Public Works and Interior and Insular Affairs Committees. He now serves on the powerful Ways and Means Committee, which oversees all the ways the government raises money, such as income taxes and taxes on all imports and exports. It also oversees benefit programs such as **Social Security**, unemployment benefits, **Medicare**, and **welfare** programs. He is also a member of many *caucuses*, which are groups of congresspeople who share the same views on certain topics. Congressman Lewis is part of the Congressional Black Caucus, the Congressional Progressive Caucus, the

21st Century Health Care Caucus, and the Gun Violence Prevention Task Force.

The most important work of Congress is to pass laws, and Congressman Lewis has been a sponsor or cosponsor of many bills that have been introduced during his time in the US House of Representatives. Bills he introduced that became law include:

- Designating a federal building in Atlanta as the Martin Luther King, Jr. Federal Building (1988)
- King Holiday and Service Act of 1994, expanding the mission of the holiday as a day of community service, interracial cooperation, and youth antiviolence **initiatives**
- National Museum of African American History and Culture Act (2003), which authorized funding for the museum in Washington, DC
- Martin Luther King, Jr. National Historic Site Land Exchange Act (2004), which established a site for the Martin Luther King, Jr. memorial in Atlanta, GA

- Emmett Till Unsolved Civil Rights Crime Act of 2007, which provided funds for the investigation of unsolved civil rights crimes.

His special interests include civil rights, equal rights (including gay rights), welfare rights, and immigrant rights. He is not afraid to engage in nonviolent actions in support of the causes in which he believes. For example, in 2013 he was one of eight Democratic lawmakers who were arrested on the National Mall in Washington, DC, where thousands rallied in support of immigrant rights. He tweeted that it was his 45th arrest. In 2016 he led fellow Democrats in a sit-in on the floor of the US House of Representatives to demand that the House pass stronger gun-control laws. And on March 14, 2018, he met with students who participated in the National School Walkout in the nation's capital. The **walkout** marked the one-month anniversary of the mass shooting at Marjorie Stoneman Douglas High School in Parkland, Florida.

Congressman Lewis is often called an "icon" of the Civil Rights Movement. More than a hero, an icon is someone who symbolizes or stands for something. He wears the icon label proudly, and as the only remaining "Big Six" civil rights leader, he feels a responsibility to keep the memory of the movement alive. Every year he returns to Selma, Alabama, to walk across the Edmund Pettus Bridge on the anniversary of the first attempt at a Selma-to-Montgomery March. He has written three bestselling, award-winning graphic novels for young people so that they will know his story. He says, "I think there's still a need for people in high places, not just in government, but in the private sector, in the academic community, in the media, in business to continue to be **advocates**, bringing people together, and build what Martin Luther King Jr. called 'the beloved community.'"

John Lewis participates in the March for Our Lives
in Atlanta, GA on March 24, 2018.

TIMELINE

1940 February 21: Born near Troy, Alabama

1955 December 5–December 21, 1956: Bus boycott in Montgomery, Alabama, which led to US Supreme Court decision declaring segregation on public transportation illegal

1956 Denied library card from Pike County (Alabama) Public Library

1957 Graduated from Pike County Training School, Brundidge, Alabama

1961 Joined Student Nonviolent Coordinating Committee (SNCC)

Participated in Freedom Rides that challenged segregation at interstate bus terminals

Graduated from American Baptist Theological Seminary, Nashville, Tennessee

1963 Elected chairman of SNCC

Graduated from Fisk University, Nashville, Tennessee, with BA degree in religion and philosophy

August 28: Spoke at Lincoln Memorial during

March on Washington for Jobs and Freedom; an estimated 250,000 people attended

1964 Coordinated SNCC voter registration drives during Mississippi Freedom Summer project

July 2: Civil Rights Act, which prohibits discrimination in public facilities, government, and employment, signed into law

1965 March 7: With Reverend Hosea Williams, led first Selma-to-Montgomery March across the Edmund Pettus Bridge, which culminated in Bloody Sunday

March 21–March 25: With other civil rights leaders, led second Selma-to-Montgomery March for voting rights; 25,000 people participated

August 6: Voting Rights Act, which provides for federal registration of voters and guaranteed every citizen the right to vote, signed into law

1966 Resigned as chairman of SNCC; continued civil rights work as associate director of the Field Foundation

1967 Appointed director of Southern Regional Council's Community Organization Project

1968 December: Married Lillian Miles

1970 Appointed executive director of Southern Regional Council's Voter Education Project (VEP)

1976 May: Son John Miles Lewis born

1977 Appointed to head ACTION, the federal volunteer agency, by President Jimmy Carter

1981 Elected to city council of Atlanta, Georgia

1986 November 4: Elected to the US House of Representatives as a Democrat from Georgia's Fifth Congressional District; reelected every two years since then

1998 *Walking with the Wind: A Memoir of the Movement*, Lewis's story of the Civil Rights Movement, published

   Presented with library card by Pike County Public Library

2001 Received John F. Kennedy Profile in Courage Award for Lifetime Achievement in recognition of his career marked by courage, leadership, vision, and commitment to human rights

2004 The John R. Lewis Monument was unveiled in Selma at the foot of the Edmund Pettus Bridge to commemorate the events of Bloody Sunday

2009   Arrested outside the Embassy of Sudan while protesting the obstruction of aid to refugees in Darfur

2011   Received the Presidential Medal of Freedom from President Barack Obama

2012   *Across That Bridge: Life Lessons and a Vision for Change* published

December 31: Lillian Miles Lewis passed away

2013   Published *March*, the first book in a graphic-novel trilogy for young adults; the second and third books were released in 2015 and 2016

2014   The film *Selma* was released, dramatizing the Selma-to-Montgomery Marches and the events surrounding them, with John Lewis as a major character

2015   March 6–7: Returned to Selma, Alabama, for the 50th anniversary of Bloody Sunday

2016   Led a sit-in on the floor of the US House of Representatives to protest inaction on gun control

2018   Published *Run*, a sequel to the March trilogy, following the events in Lewis's life after the passage of the Civil Rights Act

GLOSSARY

Abernathy, Ralph David (AB-ur-NATH-ee, Ralf DAY-vid; 1926–1990) *person* a minister and civil rights activist who led the Southern Christian Leadership Conference after the death of Martin Luther King, Jr.

advocate (AD-voh-kit) *noun* one who supports, defends, or argues for the cause of another; *verb* to act as an advocate

anxious (AINK-shuss) *adjective* worried, fearful, or excited

Baker, Ella (BAY-ker, ELL-uh; 1903–1986) *person* a long-time civil rights organizer who advised SNCC and the Mississippi Freedom Democratic Party, which pushed the Democratic Party to open up to women and minorities

"Big Six" (big siks) *plural noun* the six black civil rights leaders who coordinated and spoke at the March on Washington: James Farmer, Jr.; Martin Luther King, Jr.; John Lewis; Asa Philip Randolph; Roy Wilkins; and Whitney Young, Jr.

Black Belt of Alabama (blahk behlt uv al-uh-BAH-muh) *place* a region of southern Alabama known first for its fertile black topsoil and later its predominantly African American population

boycott (BOI-kot) *verb* to express disapproval of a person, company, or country by refusing to engage with them, especially by refusing to buy their products; *noun* the act of boycotting

bullhorn (BULL-horn) *noun* a handheld device that makes a speaker's voice louder

Carmichael, Stokely (KAR-mike-ull, STOKE-lee; 1941–1998) *person* an activist who worked for SNCC, popularized the idea of "black power," briefly led the Black Panther Party, and later changed his name to Kwame Ture and worked for pan-African liberation

civil rights (SIV-ull rites) *plural noun* the non-political rights of a citizen, including the right to privacy, freedom of speech, freedom of religion, and protection from discrimination on the basis of race, gender identity, or sexual orientation

colonial (kuh-loh-NEE-ull) *adjective* of or relating to a colony, that is, a territory established in one country through invasion and takeover from another country

concussion (kun-KUSH-un) *noun* a brain injury usually resulting from a hard blow or other impact

Congress of Racial Equality (kon-GRESS uv RAI-shull ee-KWA-leh-tee) *organization* a civil rights organization founded in 1942 that sponsored Freedom Rides and worked for desegregation

congressional district (kon-GRESH-un-ull DIS-trikt) *noun* a set area of land whose residents elect a congressperson to the national House of Representatives every two years. There are 435 congressional districts in the United States, determined by population; each district represents a little over 700,000 people

contort (kon-TORT) *verb* to bend or twist in an unnatural manner

dignity (dig-nuh-tee) *noun* seriousness; worthiness of respect

dilemma (duh-LEH-muh) *noun* circumstances in which someone must choose between two difficult options

discrimination (dis-KRIM-uh-nay-shun) *noun* the act of treating some people better than others, often for a prejudiced or unfair reason

dismay (dis-MEH) *noun* distress or alarm

disperse (dih-SPURSE) *verb* to scatter or spread about

drawback (DRAW-bak) *noun* a negative feature

economy (ee-KON-uh-mee) *noun* a system of managing and regulating resources, particularly a country's financial resources

eligible (EL-eh-juh-bull) *adjective* suitable; qualified

excerpt (ek-SURPT) *verb* to quote a passage from a longer work

Farmer, Jr., James (FARM-ur, JOON-your, James; 1920–1999) *person* an activist who cofounded the Congress of Racial Equality and organized the 1961 Freedom Rides; one of the "Big Six"

fasting (FAS-ting) *noun* the act of refusing food and water, often to draw attention to a cause

fiery (FIE-uh-ree) *adjective* spirited; fierce; passionate

Freedom Rides (FREE-dum rides) *proper noun* a series of bus trips taken throughout 1961 by black and white civil rights activists who sat together to challenge southern segregation laws. They faced great danger, violence, and imprisonment, but ultimately succeeded in desegregating interstate buses and trains.

hamlet (HAM-let) *noun* a village

hustle (HUSS-ull) *verb* to hurry

initiative (eh-NISH-uh-tev) *noun* an initial act or vement

injustice (en-JUS-tess) *noun* unfairness

loincloth (LOYN-kloth) *noun* a cloth wrapped or tied around the hips as a garment

Medicare (MED-ee-kare) *noun* a federal program established in 1965 that provides health insurance to Americans age 65 and older and to some younger people with disabilities

National Mall (NASH-uh-nal mall) *place* a national park in Washington, DC, that stretches from the US Capitol to the Lincoln Memorial, encompassing the Washington Monument, the Vietnam Veterans Memorial, the museums of the Smithsonian Institution, and many other landmarks

passive resistance (PAS-uv ree-ZIS-tunse) *noun* the act of protesting by nonviolent means

picket (PIK-et) *verb* to protest a place (usually a business) by standing outside and discouraging others from entering

plantation (plan-TAY-shun) *noun* a large farm or estate where resident laborers plant and grow the crops

Sanskrit (SAN-skrit) *proper noun* the classical language of India

segregate (seg-ree-GATE) *verb* to separate people of different groups, particularly based on race

sit-in (sit-en) *noun* a peaceful demonstration in which protesters occupy a space and refuse to leave

Social Security (SO-shull see-KYUR-eh-tee) *proper noun* a federal program established in 1935 that collects taxes from employed Americans to fund a retirement program for those who have paid into the system and are at least 62

Southern Christian Leadership Conference
(SUTH-urn KRIS-chan LEE-der-ship KON-fer-ens)
proper noun an organization founded in 1957 by more
than 60 black ministers and leaders, dedicated to
ending segregation. Martin Luther King, Jr., served
as its first president

torrent (TORE-unt) *noun* a strong flow, especially of water

unionize (YEWN-yuh-nize) *verb* to form a labor union
dedicated to bettering workers' conditions

Walker, Wyatt Tee (WALL-kur, WY-ut tee; 1928–2018)
person a minister and civil rights activist who served
as executive director of the SCLC from 1960 to 1964

walkout (WALK-out) *noun* a protest enacted by leaving an
assigned location, particularly one's work or school

welfare (WELL-fair) *noun* financial assistance given by
a government to its citizens to provide a basic stan-
dard of support

Williams, Hosea (WILL-ee-ums, Ho-ZAY-uh;
1926–2000) *person* a minister in Dr. King's inner
circle who served as an on-the-ground leader for
many major civil rights actions

Young, Andrew (Yung, An-DROO; 1932–) *person* a
minister and civil rights leader who later served
in Congress, as the US ambassador to the United
Nations, and mayor of Atlanta

TEXT SOURCES

The Atlantic. "A Sit-In on the House Floor Over Gun Control." June 22, 2016. https://www.theatlantic.com/liveblogs/2016/06/house-democrats-gun-control-sit-in/488264/

CNN.com. "John Lewis Fast Facts." Updated February 28, 2018. https://www.cnn.com/2013/02/22/us/john-lewis-fast-facts/index.html

Congress.gov. "Legislation Sponsored or Cosponsored by John Lewis." https://www.congress.gov/member/john-lewis/L000287?q=%7B%22spons/orship%22%3A%22sponsored%22%7D&page=3

Govtrack.us. "Rep. John Lewis." https://www.govtrack.us/congress/members/john_lewis/400240

Haskins, James. *Distinguished African American Political and Governmental Leaders*. Phoenix, AZ: Oryx Press, 1999.

Johnlewis.house.gov. "John Lewis." https://johnlewis.house.gov/john-lewis

Lewis, John. "The Living Legacy and Influence of Dr. Martin Luther King, Jr." Sermon at Urban Ministry Conference, First Presbyterian Church of Atlanta, Georgia, January 18, 2003.

———. Transcript of Interview with Jim Haskins, May 6, 2004.

Lewis, John, with Michael D'Orso. *Walking with the Wind: A Memoir of the Movement.* New York: Simon & Schuster, 1998.

NBC News. "Democratic lawmakers arrested during immigration protest." October 8, 2013. http://nbcpolitics.nbcnews.com/_news/2013/10/08/20874725-democratic-lawmakers-arrested-during-immigration-protest?lite

Pazzanese, Christina. "John Lewis urges: Back 'the beloved community'." *Harvard Gazette.* April 17, 2017. https://news.harvard.edu/gazette/story/2017/04/civil-rights-icon-john-lewis-headed-to-harvard-sees-work-ahead-to-guarantee-rights/

Stolberg, Cheryl Gay. "Still Marching on Washington, 50 Years Later." *The New York Times*, August 13, 2003. http://www.nytimes.com/2013/08/14/us/politics/50-years-later-fighting-the-same-civil-rights-battle.html

Voices of Democracy: The US Oratory Project. "John Lewis Speech at the March on Washington." http://voicesofdemocracy.umd.edu/john-lewis-speech-at-the-march-on-washington-28-august-1963/

SIDEBAR SOURCES

SHARECROPPING

Pollard, Samuel. *Slavery by Another Name*. Premiered
in 2012 on PBS. http://www.pbs.org/tpt/
slavery-by-another-name/home/

MOHANDAS K. GANDHI AND NONVIOLENT RESISTANCE

Encyclopedia Britannica. "Satyagraha." Updated
January 19, 2015. https://www.britannica.com/topic/
satyagraha-philosophy

Haskins, James. *The Life and Death of Martin Luther King, Jr.*
New York: Lothrop, Lee & Shepard, 1977.

History.com staff. "Mohandas Gandhi." History.
com. 2010. http://www.history.com/topics/
mahatma-gandhi

STUDENT NONVIOLENT COORDINATING COMMITTEE

Carson, Clayborne, ed. *Civil Rights Chronicle: The African
American Struggle for Freedom*. Lindenwood, IL: Legacy
Publishing, 2003.

Murray, Jonathan. "Greensboro Sit-In." North Carolina
History Project. http://northcarolinahistory.org/
encyclopedia/greensboro-sit-in/

North Carolina History Project. "SNCC (Student
     Nonviolent Coordinating Committee)." https://
     northcarolinahistory.org/encyclopedia/
     sncc-student-nonviolent-coordinating-committee/

THE BLACK CHURCH AND THE CIVIL RIGHTS MOVEMENT

Mellowes, Marilyn. "The Black Church." God in
     America: The Black Church. http://www.pbs.org/
     godinamerica/black-church/

National Park Service. "Brown Chapel AME Church."
     We Shall Overcome: Historic Places in the Civil
     Rights Movement. https://www.nps.gov/nr/travel/
     civilrights/al2.htm

RECOMMENDED FURTHER READING

Fiction books are marked with an asterisk.

Bausum, Ann. *Freedom Riders: John Lewis and Jim Zwerg on the Front Lines of the Civil Rights Movement.* Washington, DC: National Geographic Children's Books, 2005.

Bowers, Rick. *Spies of Mississippi: The True Story of the Spy Network that Tried to Destroy the Civil Rights Movement.* Washington, DC: National Geographic Children's Books, 2010.

* Curtis, Christopher Paul. *The Watsons Go to Birmingham—1963.* New York: Delacorte Books for Young Readers, 1995.

Hoose, Philip. *Claudette Colvin: Twice Toward Justice.* New York: Melanie Kroupa Books/Farrar, Straus & Giroux Books for Young Readers, 2009.

* Jackson, Linda Williams. *Midnight without a Moon.* New York: Houghton Mifflin Harcourt, 2017.

* ———. *A Sky Full of Stars.* New York: Houghton Mifflin Harcourt, 2018.

* Kelkar, Supriya. *Ahimsa.* New York: Tu Books/Lee & Low Books, 2017.

Levine, Ellen S. *Freedom's Children: Young Civil Rights Activists Tell Their Own Stories*. New York: Putnam Juvenile Books, 1993.

Lewis, John, and Andrew Aydin. *March: Book One*. Illustrated by Nate Powell. Marietta, GA: Top Shelf Productions, 2013.

————. *March: Book Two*. Illustrated by Nate Powell. Marietta, GA: Top Shelf Productions, 2015.

————. *March: Book Three*. Illustrated by Nate Powell. Marietta, GA: Top Shelf Productions, 2016.

————. *Run: Book One*. Illustrated by Nate Powell and Afua Richardson. Marietta, GA: Top Shelf Productions, 2018.

Lowery, Lynda Blackmon, as told to Elspeth Leacock and Susan Buckley. *Turning 15 on the Road to Freedom: My Story of the Selma Voting Rights March*. Illustrated by PJ Loughran. New York: Dial Books for Young Readers/ Penguin Random House, 2015.

* Magoon, Kekla. *The Rock and the River*. New York: Simon & Schuster Books for Young Readers, 2009.

Mitchell, Don. *The Freedom Summer Murders*. New York: Scholastic Press, 2014.

* Wiles, Deborah. *Revolution*. New York: Scholastic Press, 2014.

ABOUT THE AUTHORS AND ILLUSTRATOR

JIM HASKINS was the celebrated author of more than one hundred books, most on topics of African American history and achievement. His works received numerous honors, including the Coretta Scott King Author Award and the Carter G. Woodson Award. In 1994 Haskins was the recipient of the Washington Post Children's Book Guild Award for a body of work in nonfiction for young people.

KATHLEEN BENSON long served as the Curator of Community Projects at the Museum of the City of New York. With her late husband, Jim Haskins, she co-authored some twenty books for children, young adults, and adults. She lives in New York City. Find her online at kathleenbenson.com.

AARON BOYD has illustrated numerous picture books, including *Calling the Water Drum*, *Janna and the Kings*, and *Babu's Song* for Lee & Low Books. His work has been recognized by the Children's Africana Book Award and the International Literacy Association (ILA). He lives in Milwaukee, Wisconsin. You can visit him online at aaronboydart.blogspot.com.